D0688747

easy

Healthy

LOVE FOOD

Love Food ® is an imprint of Parragon Books Ltd

Parragon
Queen Street House
4 Queen Street
Bath BA1 1HE, UK

Copyright © Parragon Books Ltd 2007

Love Food ® and the accompanying heart device is a trademark of Parragon Books Ltd

Additional photography by Mike Cooper
Additional food styling by Lincoln Jefferson and Sumi Glass
Introduction written by Anne Sheasby

All rights reserved. No part of this publication may be reproduced, stored in a retrieval system
or transmitted, in any form or by any means, electronic, mechanical, photocopying, recording, or
otherwise, without the prior permission of the copyright holder.

ISBN 978-1-4075-6791-4
Printed in Indonesia

NOTES FOR THE READER
• This book uses imperial, metric, and US cup measurements. Follow the same units of measurement
throughout; do not mix imperial and metric. All spoon measurements are level, unless otherwise
stated: teaspoons are assumed to be 5 ml, and tablespoons are assumed to be 15 ml. Unless
otherwise stated, milk is assumed to be whole, eggs, and individual fruits such as bananas are
medium, and pepper is freshly ground black pepper.
• Recipes using raw or very lightly cooked eggs should be avoided by children, the elderly, pregnant
women, convalescents, and anyone with a chronic condition.
• Sufferers from nut allergies should be aware that some of the ready-prepared ingredients in the
recipes in this book may contain nuts. Pregnant and breast-feeding women are advised to avoid
eating peanuts and peanut products.
• Vegans should be aware that some of the ready-prepared ingredients in the recipes in this book may
be derived from animal products.
• Vegetarians should be aware that some of the ready-prepared ingredients in the recipes in this book
may contain meat or meat products.

Nutritional information is given per serving.

Readers are advised that the salt amounts shown per recipe do not take into account any salt which
may be added to taste, or at the table.

Contents

Introduction

Eating a balanced and varied diet is important for good health. A healthy diet will supply the correct amount of energy and nutrients that your body needs, and combined with regular exercise, it will help you to feel healthier and more energetic. Eating well can also help to reduce the risk of developing illnesses such as heart disease, some cancers, stroke, diabetes, and osteoporosis.

Fruit and vegetables should make up about one third of your food intake—aim to eat at least five portions of different fruit and vegetables each day (excluding potatoes). A portion is approximately 2½ oz/70 g (e.g. 3 heaping tablespoons peas, 2 satsumas, or 1 medium apple).

As well as fruit and vegetables, starchy carbohydrate foods should also provide about one third of your food intake. In addition, moderate amounts of meat, poultry, fish, eggs, dairy products, and vegetarian alternatives, and limited amounts of foods containing fat or sugar, should make up the rest of your diet. Drinking enough fluids is just as important as the food you eat. Aim for 6–8 glasses of water or other fluids every day.

Carbohydrates

Carbohydrates provide us with a vital supply of energy (calories) and at least half the energy in our diet should come from carbohydrates. Carbohydrates can be classified as either simple carbohydrates (such as sugars and sugary foods) or starchy, complex carbohydrates (such as potatoes, pasta, rice, bread, and other cereals).

Starchy carbohydrate foods should form the bulk of the carbohydrates we eat as they result in a slow release of energy. Whole-grain varieties also provide some dietary fiber and essential vitamins, such as B vitamins, as well as some minerals. Simple carbohydrates should be limited as they provide us with fast-release energy and no nutrients.

Sugars

High-sugar foods, such as cakes, cookies, chocolate, desserts, and sweet pastries should be eaten only occasionally as part of a healthy balanced diet.

Fats

Fat provides energy and essential fatty acids. A small amount of fat in the diet is essential for good health, but too much fat can lead to health problems such as obesity, heart disease, and diabetes.

It is important to limit your overall fat intake, particularly of saturated fat, as this is linked to an increased risk of heart disease.

Proteins

Proteins, which are made up of compounds called amino acids, are needed for the growth, maintenance, and repair of all body cells. Protein is provided by many foods including meat, poultry, fish, beans and legumes, nuts, seeds, eggs, dairy products such as cheese, milk, and yogurt, and so on.

Dietary Fiber

High-fiber foods help to keep our digestive systems healthy and can offer protection from bowel cancer. Foods rich in dietary fiber include whole wheat bread, whole wheat pasta, brown rice, whole grain breakfast cereals, oats, beans and lentils, fruit and vegetables, etc.

Vitamins & Minerals

Vitamins and minerals have many important roles in helping our bodies to function properly, including maintaining a healthy immune system, helping to protect against and prevent disease, keeping the nervous system and other tissues healthy, strengthening bones and teeth, helping to maintain healthy eyes, skin, and hair, and so on.

Salt

Some salt is needed for the body to function properly, but many of us eat too much salt. A high intake of salt in the diet will increase the risk of high blood pressure, which in turn may lead to heart disease and strokes.

Use salt sparingly (or preferably not at all) when cooking and serving food (or choose a reduced-sodium salt alternative) and try seasoning foods with other flavorings such as herbs and spices. When buying food, especially processed foods, read the food labels on the packaging carefully and be aware of the quantity of salt in foods.

Guideline Daily Amounts (GDAs)

GDAs are daily guidelines for energy and some essential nutrients, for healthy adults. They are often listed on packaged food labels to help people make sense of the nutritional labeling. They are designed to help you understand what contribution a certain food makes to your overall daily diet.

EACH DAY	MEN	WOMEN
Calories	2500	2000
Total Fat	95g	70g
Saturated Fat	30g	20g
Total Sugars	120g	90g
Dietary Fiber	24g	24g
Salt	6g	6g

Soups &
Salads

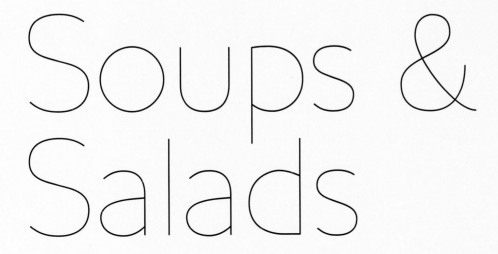

Sweet Red Bell Pepper & Tomato Soup

serves 4

1 tbsp olive oil

2 tbsp water

2 red bell peppers, deseeded and finely chopped

1 garlic clove, finely chopped

1 onion, finely chopped

14 oz/400 g canned chopped tomatoes

5 cups vegetable stock

salt and pepper

fresh basil leaves, to garnish

Put the oil, water, bell peppers, garlic, and onion in a pan, heat gently, and cook for 5–10 minutes, or until the vegetables have softened. Cover the pan and simmer for a further 10 minutes.

Add the tomatoes, stock, salt, and pepper and simmer, uncovered, for 15 minutes.

Serve garnished with basil leaves.

Calories: 89   Fat: 4g   Sat Fat: 0.5g   Salt: 0.4g

Roast Mushroom & Garlic Soup with Whole Wheat Croûtons

serves 1

2 open-cap mushrooms

2 garlic cloves

1 slice whole wheat bread, cut into small cubes

1 tsp olive oil

2 tbsp dried porcini mushrooms

generous 1 cup vegetable stock

1 tsp fresh thyme leaves

1 tsp vegetarian Worcestershire sauce

1 tsp half-fat crème fraîche, (optional)

pepper

few fresh thyme sprigs, to garnish

Preheat the oven to 350°F/180°C. Loosely wrap the open-cap mushrooms and garlic in foil and place in the oven. Bake for 10 minutes, open the foil, and bake for 5 minutes more.

To prepare the croûtons, drizzle the bread cubes with the olive oil on a cookie sheet and bake for 10–15 minutes, or until golden brown.

Meanwhile, put the porcini mushrooms, stock, and thyme leaves in a pan with a lid. When the open-cap mushrooms are cooked, remove them from the oven, unwrap, slice, and add them to the pan with the Worcestershire sauce, roasted garlic, and the mushroom juices. Season with pepper. Cover and simmer for 15 minutes over low heat.

Let cool slightly and process half the soup in a blender for a few seconds. Return to the pan and reheat gently. Stir in the crème fraîche, if using, and adjust the seasoning to taste. Transfer to a bowl, sprinkle with the croûtons and sprigs of thyme, and serve.

Calories: 140   Fat: 5.4g   Sat Fat: 1.2g   Salt: 1.0g

Carrot & Cumin Soup

serves 1–2

1 medium to large carrot, finely chopped

1 small garlic clove, chopped

1 medium to large shallot, finely chopped

1 ripe tomato, skinned and chopped

½ tsp ground cumin, plus extra to garnish

scant 1 cup vegetable stock

1 bouquet garni

2 tsp dry sherry (optional)

pepper

1 tbsp half-fat crème fraîche (optional), to serve

Put all the ingredients, except the sherry and crème fraîche, in a pan with a lid. Bring to simmering point over high heat, then reduce the heat, cover, and simmer for 30 minutes, or until the vegetables are tender.

Cool slightly and remove the bouquet garni. Pour the soup into a blender and process until smooth. Return to the pan, add the sherry, if using, and reheat. Season to taste with pepper. Serve with a swirl of crème fraîche, if using, garnished with a pinch of cumin.

Calories: 135   Fat: 1g   Sat Fat: 0.1g   Salt: 0.1g

Speedy Broccoli Soup

serves 6

12 oz/350 g head of broccoli

1 leek, sliced

1 celery stalk, sliced

1 garlic clove, crushed

12 oz/350 g potato, diced

4 cups vegetable stock

1 bay leaf

freshly ground black pepper

crusty bread or toasted croûtons, to serve

Cut the broccoli into florets and set aside. Cut the thicker broccoli stalks into ½-inch/1-cm dice and put into a large pan with the leek, celery, garlic, potato, stock, and bay leaf. Bring to a boil, then reduce the heat, cover, and let simmer for 15 minutes.

Add the broccoli florets to the soup and return to a boil. Reduce the heat, cover, and let simmer for an additional 3–5 minutes, or until the potato and broccoli stalks are tender.

Remove from the heat and let the soup cool slightly. Remove and discard the bay leaf. Purée the soup, in small batches, in a food processor or blender until smooth.

Return the soup to the pan and heat through thoroughly. Season to taste with pepper. Ladle the soup into warmed bowls and serve at once with crusty bread or toasted croûtons.

Calories: 140	Fat: 1.3g	Sat Fat: 0.27g	Salt: 0.1g

Spiced Lentil & Vegetable Soup

serves 1

1 tsp vegetable or olive oil

1 tsp mild curry paste

1 garlic clove, crushed or finely chopped

1½ cups vegetable stock

1 onion, chopped

2½ tbsp red lentils

1 carrot, chopped

1 small parsnip or potato, chopped

1 celery stalk, chopped

1 tsp tomato paste

Heat the oil in a nonstick pan with a lid, add the curry paste and garlic, and stir over low heat for 1 minute. Add the stock and stir to combine, then add the remaining ingredients, and bring to a simmer over medium-high heat.

Reduce the heat, cover, and cook for 40–50 minutes, or until the lentils are tender. Remove half or all the soup from the pan and process in a blender. Return the soup to the pan and reheat gently to serve.

| Calories: 280 | Fat: 1.4g | Sat Fat: 0.1g | Salt: 0.8g |

Speedy Minestrone Soup

serves 4

2 sprays olive oil

1 onion, finely chopped

1 large carrot, about
4 oz/115 g, peeled and
diced

2 celery stalks, trimmed
and sliced

1 bouquet garni

14 oz/400 g canned
chopped tomatoes

2 oz/55 g dried soup pasta
shells or spaghetti
broken into short lengths

3½ cups vegetable stock

½ small cabbage, about
8 oz/225 g

pepper

Heat the oil in a large pan, add the onion, carrot, and celery and sauté gently for 5 minutes, stirring frequently. Add the bouquet garni with the tomatoes. Half-fill the empty tomato can with water, swirl to remove all the remaining tomatoes, then pour into the pan.

Add the pasta with the stock and bring to a boil. Reduce the heat to a simmer and cook for 12 minutes, or until the vegetables are almost tender.

Discard any outer leaves and hard central core from the cabbage and shred. Wash well, then add to the pan with pepper to taste. Continue to cook for 5–8 minutes, or until all the vegetables are tender, but still firm to the bite. Serve divided equally among 4 warmed bowls.

Calories: 91   Fat: 2.0g   Sat Fat: 0.3g   Salt: 0.2g

Sweet Potato & Garlic Soup

serves 4

1 whole garlic bulb

2 sprays olive oil

1 onion, chopped

10½ oz/300 g sweet potatoes, peeled and chopped

4 cups vegetable stock

4 oz/115 g green string beans, trimmed and finely chopped

pepper

1 tbsp snipped fresh chives

4 tbsp low-fat plain yogurt, to serve

Preheat the oven to 375°F/190°C. Pull the garlic bulb apart and put in a small roasting pan. Roast in the oven for 20 minutes, or until softened. Remove and let cool before squeezing out the soft insides. Set aside.

Heat the oil in a heavy-bottom pan, add the onion and sweet potato, and cook, stirring continuously, for 5 minutes. Add the stock and bring to a boil. Cover with a lid, reduce the heat, and simmer for 10 minutes. Add the beans and the roasted garlic flesh and continue to simmer for 10 minutes, or until the potatoes are tender. Remove and let cool slightly.

Set aside 2 tablespoons of the cooked beans, then pass the soup through a food processor and return to the rinsed-out pan. Add the reserved beans with pepper to taste and heat through for 3 minutes.

Ladle the soup into warmed bowls, swirl a spoonful of yogurt in each and sprinkle with snipped chives. Serve immediately.

Calories: 287   Fat: 4.7g   Sat Fat: 0.8g   Salt: 0.2g

Miso Fish Soup

serves 4

3½ cups fish stock or vegetable stock

1-inch/2.5-cm piece fresh ginger, peeled and grated

1 tbsp mirin or dry sherry

1 fresh Thai chile, seeded and finely sliced

1 carrot, about 3 oz/85 g, peeled and thinly sliced

2 oz/55 g daikon, peeled and cut into thin strips or ½ bunch radishes, trimmed and sliced

1 yellow bell pepper, seeded and cut into thin strips

3 oz/85 g shiitake mushrooms, sliced if large

1½ oz/40 g thread egg noodles

8 oz/225 g sole fillets, skinned and cut into strips

1 tbsp miso paste

4 scallions, trimmed and shredded

Pour the stock into a large pan and add the ginger, mirin, and chile. Bring to a boil, then reduce the heat, and simmer for 5 minutes.

Add the carrot with the daikon, bell pepper strips, mushrooms, and noodles and simmer for an additional 3 minutes.

Add the fish strips with the miso paste and continue to cook for 2 minutes, or until the fish is tender. Top with the scallions and serve.

Calories: 274   Fat: 4.8g   Sat Fat: 0.9g   Salt: 0.8g

Chicken & Vegetable Soup

serves 4

1 onion, finely chopped

1 garlic clove, finely chopped

1¼ cups shredded white cabbage

2 medium carrots, finely chopped

4 potatoes, diced

1 green bell pepper, seeded and diced

14 oz/400 g canned chopped tomatoes

5⅔ cups chicken stock

1¼ cups diced cooked chicken

salt and pepper

chopped fresh flat-leaf parsley, to garnish

Put all the ingredients, except the chicken and parsley, in a large pan and bring to a boil. Simmer for 1 hour, or until the vegetables are tender.

Add the chicken and simmer for a further 10 minutes, or until hot.

Garnish with parsley and serve.

Calories: 240   Fat: 3g   Sat Fat: 0.5g   Salt: 0.4g

Lentil & Goat Cheese Salad

serves 1

2 tbsp Puy lentils

1 bay leaf

2 scallions, finely chopped

scant ¼ cup diced red bell pepper

1 tbsp chopped fresh parsley

3½ oz/100 g cherry tomatoes, halved

⅓ cup arugula

1 oz/25 g goat cheese, sliced or crumbled

for the dressing

1 tsp olive oil

1 tsp balsamic vinegar

½ tsp honey

1 garlic clove, crushed or finely chopped

Rinse the lentils and put in a medium-size pan. Add the bay leaf and cover with plenty of cold water. Bring to a boil, then reduce the heat, and simmer for 20–30 minutes, or until the lentils are tender.

Drain the lentils and transfer to a bowl. Add the scallions, bell pepper, parsley, and cherry tomatoes. Mix well.

To make the dressing, whisk together the oil, vinegar, honey, and garlic and stir into the lentils. Serve on a bed of arugula, sprinkled with the goat cheese.

Calories: 220   Fat: 9.3g   Sat Fat: 3.8g   Salt: 0.4g

Fruity Cottage Cheese Salad

serves 4

⅓ cup cottage cheese

1 tsp chopped fresh parsley

1 tbsp snipped fresh chives

1 tsp chopped fresh chervil or basil

2 assorted colored bell peppers, seeded and peeled

1 small melon, such as ogen (about 10½ oz/ 300 g after peeling and seeding)

6 oz/175 g assorted salad greens

2 oz/55 g seedless grapes

1 red onion, thinly sliced

for the dressing

3 tbsp freshly squeezed lime juice

1 small fresh red chile, seeded and finely chopped

1 tsp honey

1 tbsp soy sauce

Place the cottage cheese in a bowl and stir in the chopped herbs. Cover lightly and set aside.

Cut the peeled bell peppers into thin strips and set aside. Cut the melon in half, discard the seeds and cut into small wedges. Remove and discard the rind, or run a sharp knife between the skin and flesh to loosen, then cut the flesh horizontally across. Push the flesh in alternate directions but so that it still sits on the skin. Set aside.

Arrange the salad greens on a large serving platter with the melon wedges.

Spoon the herb-flavored cottage cheese on the platter and arrange the reserved bell peppers, the grapes, and red onion slices around the cheese.

To make the dressing, mix the lime juice, chile, honey, and soy sauce together in a small bowl or pitcher then drizzle over the salad and serve as 4 portions.

| Calories: 83 | Fat: 1.5g | Sat Fat: 0.6g | Salt: 0.9g |

Warm Oriental-Style Salad

serves 4

4 oz/115 g broccoli florets

4 oz/115 g baby carrots, scraped and cut in half lengthwise

5 oz/140 g bok choy

2 sprays sunflower oil

1 red onion, sliced

1–2 fresh Thai chiles, seeded and sliced

1-inch/2.5-cm piece fresh ginger, peeled and grated

2 whole star anise

1 red bell pepper, seeded and cut into strips

1 orange bell pepper, seeded and cut into strips

4 oz/115 g baby zucchini, trimmed and sliced diagonally

4 oz/115 g baby corn, sliced in half lengthwise

2 tbsp orange juice

1 tbsp soy sauce

1 tbsp cashew nuts

Cut the broccoli into tiny florets, then bring a small pan of water to a boil, and add the halved carrots. Cook for 3 minutes then add the broccoli and cook for an additional 2 minutes. Drain and plunge into cold water, then drain again, and set aside.

Arrange 1 oz/25 g of bok choy on a large serving platter. Shred the remainder and set aside.

Heat a wok and when hot, add the oil and heat for 30 seconds. Add the sliced onion, chiles, ginger, and star anise and stir-fry for 1 minute. Add the bell pepper strips, zucchini, and baby corn and stir-fry for an additional 2 minutes.

Pour in the orange juice and soy sauce and continue to stir-fry for an additional 1 minute before adding the reserved shredded bok choy. Stir-fry for 2 minutes, or until the vegetables are tender but still firm to the bite. Arrange the warm salad on the bok choy-lined serving platter, scatter the cashew nuts over the top, and serve as 4 portions.

| Calories: 106 | Fat: 4.0g | Sat Fat: 0.8g | Salt: 0.7g |

Greek Feta Salad

serves 4

4 tomatoes, sliced

½ cucumber, peeled and sliced

1 small red onion, sliced thinly

4 oz/115 g feta cheese, cubed

8 black olives

a few grape leaves

for the dressing

3 tbsp extra virgin olive oil

1 tbsp lemon juice

½ tsp dried oregano

salt and pepper

To make the dressing, put the oil, lemon juice, oregano, salt, and pepper in a screw-topped jar and shake together until blended.

Arrange the grape leaves on a serving dish and then the tomatoes, cucumber, and onion. Sprinkle the cheese and olives on top. Pour the dressing over the salad and serve.

| Calories: 186 | Fat: 15g | Sat Fat: 6.0g | Salt: 0.7g |

Warm Duck Salad

serves 4

6 oz/175 g duck breast, all fat removed

2–3 sprays sunflower oil

1-inch/2.5-cm piece fresh ginger, peeled and grated

1 fresh serrano chile, seeded and sliced

1 red onion, cut into thin wedges

2 celery stalks, trimmed and finely sliced

1 small red bell pepper, seeded and finely sliced

1 tbsp soy sauce

4 oz/115 g zucchini, trimmed and sliced

2 ripe but still firm plums, pitted and sliced

3 oz/85 g bok choy, shredded

1 tbsp chopped fresh cilantro

Cut the duck breast into thin strips and set aside. Heat a wok until very hot, then spray with the oil, and heat for 30 seconds. Add the ginger, chile, and duck strips and stir-fry for 1–2 minutes, or until the duck strips are browned.

Add the onion wedges, celery, and pepper slices and continue to stir-fry for 3 minutes.

Add the soy sauce, zucchini, and plums to the wok and stir-fry for 2 minutes before stirring in the shredded bok choy and the chopped cilantro. Stir-fry for an additional minute then serve, divided equally among 4 bowls.

| Calories: 129 | Fat: 6.0g | Sat Fat: 1.7g | Salt: 0.8g |

Thai Chicken Salad

serves 6

vegetable oil spray

4 oz/115 g skinless chicken breast portion, cut lengthwise horizontally

1 oz/25 g rice vermicelli

ready-made low-fat spicy dressing of your choice

3 limes, halved

for the salad

1¾ oz/50 g seeded mixed bell peppers, sliced into thin strips

⅓ cup thin carrot strips

⅓ cup thin zucchini strips

⅓ cup thin snow pea strips

scant ½ cup baby corn cobs, sliced into thin strips

½ cup broccoli florets, cut into ¼-inch/5-mm pieces

½ cup shredded bok choy

4 tbsp coarsely chopped fresh cilantro leaves

Heat a grill pan over high heat and spray lightly with oil. Add the chicken and cook for 2 minutes on each side, or until thoroughly cooked through. Remove the chicken from the pan and shred.

Cook the vermicelli according to the packet instructions.

To make the salad, put all the salad ingredients with the chicken into a large bowl. Drain the vermicelli and add to the bowl. Pour the dressing over the salad and toss together, making sure that all the ingredients are well coated. Cover and chill in the refrigerator for at least 2 hours before serving. Serve on large plates, squeezing the juice from half a lime over each serving.

| Calories: 134 | Fat: 1.5g | Sat Fat: 0.4g | Salt: 0.3g |

Warm Salmon & Mango Salad

serves 4

4 oz/115 g sungold or red cherry tomatoes

3 oz/85 g salmon fillets, skinned and cut into small cubes

1 large ripe mango (about 5 oz/140 g peeled fruit), peeled and cut into small chunks

2 tbsp orange juice

1 tbsp soy sauce

4 oz/115 g assorted salad greens

½ cucumber, trimmed and sliced into thin sticks

6 scallions, trimmed and chopped

for the dressing

4 tbsp low-fat plain yogurt

1 tsp soy sauce

1 tbsp finely grated orange rind

Soak 4 wooden skewers in a bowl of cold water for 30 minutes to prevent them burning during cooking. Cut half the tomatoes in half and set aside.

Thread the salmon with the whole tomatoes and half the mango chunks onto 4 kabob sticks. Mix the orange juice and soy sauce together in a small bowl and brush over the kabobs. Let marinate for 15 minutes, brushing with the remaining orange juice mixture at least once more.

Arrange the salad greens on a serving platter with the reserved halved tomatoes, mango chunks, the cucumber sticks, and scallions.

Preheat the broiler to high and line the broiler rack with foil. To make the dressing, mix the yogurt, soy sauce, and grated orange rind together in a small bowl and set aside.

Place the salmon kabobs on the broiler rack, brush again with the marinade, and broil for 5–7 minutes, or until the salmon is cooked. Turn the kabobs over halfway through cooking and brush with any remaining marinade.

Divide the prepared salad among 4 plates, top each with a kabob, and then drizzle with the dressing.

Calories: 95   Fat: 3.0g   Sat Fat: 0.7g   Salt: 1.4g

Spicy Warm Crab Salad

serves 4

2 sprays sunflower oil

1 fresh serrano chile, seeded and finely chopped

4 oz/115 g snow peas, cut diagonally in half

6 scallions, trimmed and finely shredded

2 heaping tbsp frozen corn kernels, defrosted

5½ oz/150 g white crabmeat, drained if canned

2 oz/55 g raw shrimp, peeled and deveined, thawed if frozen

1 carrot, about 3 oz/85 g, peeled and grated

¾ cup bean sprouts

8 oz/225 g fresh baby spinach leaves

1 tbsp finely grated orange rind

2 tbsp orange juice

1 tbsp chopped fresh cilantro, for sprinkling

Heat a wok and, when hot, spray in the oil and heat for 30 seconds. Add the chile and snow peas then stir-fry over medium heat for 2 minutes.

Add the scallions and corn and continue to stir-fry for an additional 1 minute.

Add the crabmeat, shrimp, carrot, bean sprouts, and spinach leaves. Stir in the orange rind and juice and stir-fry for 2–3 minutes, or until the spinach has begun to wilt and everything is cooked. Serve divided equally among 4 bowls, sprinkled with the chopped cilantro.

Calories: 188   Fat: 9.0g   Sat Fat: 1.7g   Salt: 1.3g

Shrimp & Rice Salad

serves 4

scant 1 cup mixed long-grain and wild rice

12 oz/350 g cooked shelled shrimp

1 mango, peeled, seeded, and diced

4 scallions, sliced

¼ cup slivered almonds

1 tbsp finely chopped fresh mint

salt and pepper

for the dressing

1 tbsp extra virgin olive oil

2 tsp lime juice

1 garlic clove, crushed

1 tsp honey

salt and pepper

Cook the rice in a large pan of lightly salted boiling water for 35 minutes, or until tender. Drain and transfer to a large bowl, then add the shrimp.

To make the dressing, mix all the ingredients together in a large measuring cup, seasoning to taste with the salt and pepper, and whisk well until thoroughly blended. Pour the dressing over the rice and shrimp mixture and let cool.

Add the mango, scallions, almonds, and mint to the salad and season to taste with pepper. Stir thoroughly and transfer to a large serving dish and serve.

Calories: 261   Fat: 7.0g   Sat Fat: 1.0g   Salt: 3.0g

Meat & Fish Mains

Chili Beef with Black-Eyed Peas

serves 1

1 tsp olive oil

1 small onion, finely chopped

1 garlic clove, crushed or finely chopped

1 small green bell pepper, seeded and chopped into ½-inch/1-cm squares

2¾ oz/75 g extra-lean braising beef, finely diced

1 tsp concentrated vegetable stock

2 tsp tomato paste

½ green chile, seeded and finely chopped

⅓ cup drained canned black-eyed peas or kidney beans, rinsed

3½ oz/100 g chopped canned tomatoes

½ tsp chili sauce

1¾ oz/50 g white rice

pepper

Heat the oil in a nonstick skillet and sauté the onion, garlic, and bell pepper over medium heat for 2–3 minutes, until the onion is softened and just turning golden.

Add the braising beef and cook, stirring, until browned on all sides. Add the remaining ingredients, except the rice, and season to taste with pepper. Stir well and bring to simmer point. Reduce the heat, cover, and cook for 30 minutes, then check the dish for heat, seasoning, and dryness. Add extra chili sauce, very finely chopped fresh chile, or chopped pickled chiles if it is not hot enough for you, and add water if the sauce looks too dry. Cook for 25–30 minutes more, until the meat is completely tender.

Meanwhile, cook the rice according to the instructions on the packet. Drain and transfer the cooked rice to a warm plate, spoon the sauce over it, and serve.

Calories: 445   Fat: 8.5g   Sat Fat: 2.1g   Salt: 1.2g

Beef Casserole with Mustard Mashed Potatoes

serves 2

2 tsp vegetable oil

8 oz/225 g extra-lean braising beef, cut into 8 pieces

10 small shallots

1 garlic clove, crushed

1 tomato, chopped

scant 1½ cups thinly sliced mushrooms

⅔ cup red wine

scant ½ cup chicken stock

1 small bouquet garni

1 tsp cornstarch

salt and pepper

for the mashed potatoes

2 mealy potatoes, sliced

1½–2 tbsp warm skim milk

1 tsp Dijon mustard

Preheat the oven to 350°F/180°C.

Heat the oil in a heavy flameproof casserole. Add the meat and shallots and cook over high heat, stirring, for 4–5 minutes, until the meat is browned on all sides.

Add the garlic, tomato, mushrooms, wine, and stock and tuck the bouquet garni in well. Bring to a simmer, cover, and transfer the casserole to the oven for 45–60 minutes, or until everything is tender.

About 30 minutes before the beef is ready, put the potatoes into a pan of boiling water and simmer for 20 minutes, or until just tender. Remove from heat, drain well, and put in a bowl. Add the milk and mash well. Stir in the mustard to taste and keep warm.

Use a slotted spoon to remove the meat and vegetables to a warm serving dish. Bring the sauce to a boil over high heat and cook until reduced by half. Reduce the heat, remove the bouquet garni, and taste and adjust the seasoning. Mix the cornstarch with a little cold water to form a paste, add to the sauce, stirring well, and bring back to a simmer. Pour the sauce over the meat and serve with the mustard mashed potatoes.

| Calories: 330 | Fat: 6.4g | Sat Fat: 1.6g | Salt: 1.3g |

The Perfect Burger

serves 4

6 oz/175 g fresh lean beef, such as round, ground

2 shallots, finely chopped

1 tbsp Worcestershire sauce, or to taste

pepper

2 sprays sunflower oil

2 onions, thinly sliced

4 beef tomatoes

1–2 garlic cloves, peeled

tomato ketchup, to serve (optional)

Put the ground beef in a bowl and add the shallots, Worcestershire sauce, and pepper to taste. Mix together and, with damp hands, shape into 4 equal-size burgers. Place the burgers on a plate, cover lightly with plastic wrap, and chill until required.

Preheat the broiler to high and line the broiler rack with foil. Heat a nonstick skillet, spray with the oil, and add the sliced onion. Cook over low heat for 12–15 minutes, stirring frequently until the onions are tender. Keep warm if necessary.

Cut the tomatoes into thick slices and the garlic cloves into slivers. Stud the tomatoes with the garlic and place on the broiler rack together with the burgers.

Cook the burgers for 3–4 minutes on each side, or according to personal preference. If the tomatoes are cooking too quickly, either remove them and add a little later or remove and keep warm. Serve each burger between the thick tomato slices with the onion garnish and ketchup, if using.

| Calories: 116 | Fat: 5.0g | Sat Fat: 3.0g | Salt: 0.2g |

Beef Stir-Fry

serves 4

2–3 sprays olive oil

5 oz/140 g beef steak, such as round (fat removed), cut into thin strips

1 orange bell pepper, seeded and cut into thin strips

4 scallions, trimmed and chopped

1–2 fresh jalapeño chiles, seeded and chopped

2–3 garlic cloves, chopped

4 oz/115 g snow peas, trimmed and cut in half diagonally

4 oz/115 g large portobello mushrooms, sliced

1–2 tsp hoisin sauce, or to taste

1 tbsp orange juice

3 oz/85 g arugula or watercress sprigs

Heat a wok then spray in the oil and heat for 30 seconds. Add the beef and stir-fry for 1 minute or until browned. Using a slotted spoon, remove and set aside.

Add the pepper, scallions, chiles, and garlic and stir-fry for 2 minutes. Add the snow peas and mushrooms and stir-fry for an additional 2 minutes.

Return the beef to the wok and add the hoisin sauce and orange juice. Stir-fry for 2–3 minutes, or until the beef is tender and the vegetables are tender but still firm to the bite. Stir in the arugula and stir-fry until it starts to wilt. Serve immediately, divided equally among 4 warmed bowls.

Calories: 103   Fat: 3.9g   Sat Fat: 1.2g   Salt: 0.6g

Spanish Rice with Pork & Peppers

serves 1

½ tsp olive oil

2¾ oz/75 g lean pork tenderloin, cut into small cubes

1 small onion or 2 shallots, finely chopped

1 garlic clove, chopped

1 red or orange bell pepper, seeded and chopped into ½-inch/1-cm squares

7 oz/200 g chopped canned tomatoes

1 tbsp chopped fresh parsley

pinch of saffron threads

⅓ cup brown basmati rice

1 cup chicken or vegetable stock

pepper

Heat the oil in a heavy nonstick skillet with a lid and brown the pork on all sides over high heat. Remove with a slotted spoon and keep warm.

Reduce the heat to medium-high, add the onion, garlic, and bell pepper, and stir-fry for a few minutes, until everything is softened and turning golden. Return the meat to the skillet, add the tomatoes, parsley, saffron, rice, and stock, and season to taste with pepper. Stir well to combine and to break up the tomatoes a little, and bring to a simmer.

Reduce the heat, cover, and simmer for 30–40 minutes, or until the rice is tender and all the stock has been absorbed. (If the rice is not cooked but the dish looks dry, add a little more hot water.)

Calories: 430   Fat: 10.2g   Sat Fat: 2.6g   Salt: 1.4g

Lamb & Mint Burgers

serves 4

1½ cups lean ground lamb

1 medium onion, finely chopped

4 tbsp dry whole wheat breadcrumbs

2 tbsp mint jelly

salt and pepper

for the dressing

4 tbsp low-fat cream cheese

1 tbsp mint jelly, softened

2-inch/5-cm piece cucumber, finely diced

1 tbsp chopped fresh mint

to serve

4 whole wheat baps, split

2 large tomatoes, sliced

small piece of cucumber, sliced

lettuce leaves

Place the lamb in a large bowl and mix in the onion, bread crumbs, and mint jelly. Season well with salt and pepper, then mold the ingredients together with your hands to form a firm mixture.

Divide the mixture into 4 portions and form each portion into a circle measuring 4 inches/10 cm across. Place the circles on a plate lined with parchment paper and let chill in the refrigerator for 30 minutes.

Preheat the broiler to medium. Line a broiler rack with foil, securing the ends under the rack, and place the burgers on top. Cook for 8 minutes, then turn the burgers over with a spatula and cook for an additional 7 minutes, or until the burgers are cooked through.

Meanwhile, make the dressing. Mix the cream cheese, mint jelly, cucumber, and chopped mint together in a small bowl. Cover with plastic wrap and let chill in the refrigerator for 1 hour, or until required.

Drain the burgers on paper towels and serve inside baps with sliced tomatoes, cucumber, lettuce, and the dressing.

| Calories: 342 | Fat: 9.6g | Sat Fat: 4.0g | Salt: 1.0g |

Seared Duck with Onion Relish

serves 4

7 oz/200 g duck breast (after all fat and skin is removed)

1 tbsp orange rind

1⅓ cups water, plus 1 extra tbsp

2 tbsp balsamic vinegar or red wine vinegar

2 sprays sunflower oil

2 red onions, very thinly sliced

2 garlic cloves, crushed

1 tsp dark brown sugar

1 tsp cornstarch

1 tbsp chopped fresh parsley and orange wedges, to garnish

Lightly rinse the duck breast, pat dry with paper towels, slice thinly, and put in a nonmetallic dish that will not react with acid.

Blend the orange rind with ⅔ cup water and 1 tablespoon of vinegar in a bowl and pour over the duck. Cover lightly with plastic wrap, and let marinate for at least 20 minutes. Stir occasionally during marinating.

Meanwhile, heat a nonstick pan and spray with the oil. Add the onions and garlic and cook, stirring, over low heat for 5 minutes. Sprinkle in the sugar, then add the remaining water and vinegar. Cover and cook for 10 minutes, or until the onions are softened. Keep warm.

Heat a nonstick heavy-bottom skillet, add the duck breasts with the marinade, and cook gently for 6 minutes. Add the cooked onions with any liquor and stir together lightly.

Blend the cornstarch with 1 tablespoon of water and stir into the skillet. Cook, stirring, until the liquid has thickened, then cook for an additional 2 minutes, or until the duck is tender and the onions are hot. Garnish with parsley and orange wedges, and serve immediately.

Calories: 128   Fat: 6.5g   Sat Fat: 1.8g   Salt: 0.1g

Chinese Lemon Chicken

serves 4

10½ oz/300 g skinless, boneless chicken breast

chopped fresh herbs, to garnish

for the marinade

⅔ cup freshly squeezed lemon juice

1 tbsp light soy sauce

1 tbsp cornstarch

Lightly rinse the chicken and pat dry with paper towels. Cut into bite-size cubes and place in a shallow dish.

Mix the lemon juice and soy sauce together in a bowl. Put the cornstarch in another bowl and stir in the lemon and soy mixture to form a paste. Spread over the chicken and let marinate for 15 minutes.

Heat a nonstick skillet and add the chicken and marinade. Cook, stirring, for 10–12 minutes, or until the chicken is thoroughly cooked. Transfer to 4 serving plates, pour over the sauce, and serve, garnished with fresh herbs.

| Calories: 93 | Fat: 0.7g | Sat Fat: 0.2g | Salt: 0.7g |

Spicy Tomato Chicken

serves 4

1 lb 2 oz/500 g skinless, boneless chicken breasts

3 tbsp tomato paste

2 tbsp honey

2 tbsp Worcestershire sauce

1 tbsp chopped fresh rosemary

9 oz/250 g cherry tomatoes

fresh rosemary sprigs, to garnish

freshly cooked couscous or rice, to serve

Using a sharp knife, cut the chicken into 1-inch/2.5-cm chunks and place in a bowl. Mix the tomato paste, honey, Worcestershire sauce, and rosemary together in a separate bowl, then add to the chicken, stirring to coat evenly.

Soak 8 wooden skewers in a bowl of cold water for 30 minutes to prevent them burning during cooking. Preheat the broiler to medium. Thread the chicken pieces and cherry tomatoes alternately onto the skewers and place on a broiler rack.

Spoon over any remaining glaze and cook under the preheated hot broiler for 8–10 minutes, turning occasionally, until the chicken is cooked through. Transfer to 4 large serving plates, garnish with a few sprigs of fresh rosemary, and serve with freshly cooked couscous or rice.

Calories: 195	Fat: 4g	Sat Fat: 0.4g	Salt: 0.5g

Moroccan-Style Turkey with Apricots

serves 4

14 oz/400 g skinless, boneless turkey breast, diced

1 onion, sliced

1 tsp ground cumin

½ tsp ground cinnamon

1 tsp hot chili pepper sauce

8½ oz/240 g canned chickpeas, drained

2½ cups chicken stock

12 dried apricots

generous ¼ cup cornstarch

generous ¼ cup cold water

2 tbsp chopped fresh cilantro

cooked couscous or rice, to serve

Put the turkey, onion, cumin, cinnamon, chili pepper sauce, chickpeas, and stock into a large pan and bring to a boil, then reduce the heat, cover, and let simmer for 15 minutes.

Stir in the apricots and return to a boil. Reduce the heat, cover, and let simmer for an additional 15 minutes, or until the turkey is thoroughly cooked and tender.

Blend the cornstarch with the water in a small bowl and stir into the casserole. Return to a boil, stirring constantly, and cook until the casserole thickens. Reduce the heat, cover, and let simmer for an additional 5 minutes.

Stir half the cilantro into the casserole. Transfer to a warmed serving dish and sprinkle over the remaining cilantro. Serve at once with cooked couscous or rice.

Calories: 387   Fat: 4.7g   Sat Fat: 1.3g   Salt: 0.8g

Curry-Topped Salmon

serves 4

4 salmon fillets, about
6 oz/175 g each

scant 1 cup fresh whole
wheat breadcrumbs

1½ tbsp curry paste

1 tbsp chopped fresh
cilantro

lemon wedges to garnish

salad greens, to serve

Preheat the oven to 350°F/180°C. Discard any fine bones from the salmon fillets and rinse lightly. Pat dry with paper towels.

Mix the breadcrumbs, curry paste, and chopped cilantro together in a bowl until well blended.

Place each salmon fillet on a sheet of foil and pat the curry-flavored breadcrumbs on top of each. Cover with another sheet of foil and place on one or two large baking sheets.

Bake for 10 minutes then remove the top sheet of foil and cook for an additional 10 minutes, or until the salmon is tender. Serve garnished with lemon wedges and serve with salad greens.

| Calories: 380 | Fat: 23.0g | Sat Fat: 3.8g | Salt: 0.4g |

Teriyaki Salmon Fillets with Chinese Noodles

serves 4

4 salmon fillets, about 7 oz/200 g each

½ cup teriyaki marinade

1 shallot, sliced

¾-inch/2-cm piece fresh ginger, finely chopped

2 carrots, sliced

4 oz/115 g closed-cup mushrooms, sliced

5 cups vegetable stock

9 oz/250 g dried medium egg noodles

1 cup frozen peas

6 oz/175 g Napa cabbage, shredded

4 scallions, sliced

Arrange the salmon, skin-side up, in a dish. Mix the teriyaki marinade with the shallot and ginger in a bowl and pour over the fish. Cover and marinate in the refrigerator for 1 hour, turning halfway through.

Put the carrots, mushrooms, and stock into a large pan. Arrange the salmon, skin-side down, on a shallow baking sheet. Pour the fish marinade into the pan of vegetables and stock and bring to a boil. Reduce the heat, cover, and let simmer for 10 minutes.

Meanwhile, preheat the broiler to medium. Cook the salmon under the preheated broiler for 10–15 minutes, depending on the thickness of the fillets, until the flesh turns pink and flakes easily. Remove from the broiler and keep warm.

Add the noodles and peas to the stock and return to a boil. Reduce the heat, cover, and let simmer for 5 minutes, or until the noodles are tender. Stir in the Napa cabbage and scallions and heat through for 1 minute.

Drain off 300 ml/10 fl oz of the stock into a jug and reserve. Drain and discard the remaining stock. Divide the noodles and vegetables between warmed bowls and top each with a salmon fillet. Pour over the reserved stock and serve.

Calories: 533   Fat: 22.4g   Sat Fat: 5.7g   Salt: 1.2g

Broiled Tuna & Vegetable Kabobs

serves 4

4 tuna steaks, about
5 oz/140 g each

2 red onions

12 cherry tomatoes

1 red bell pepper, seeded
and diced into 1-inch/
2.5-cm pieces

1 yellow bell pepper,
seeded and diced into
1-inch/2.5-cm pieces

1 zucchini, sliced

1 tbsp chopped fresh
oregano

4 tbsp olive oil

freshly ground black
pepper

lime wedges, to garnish

salad greens, to serve

Preheat the broiler to high. Cut the tuna into 1-inch/2.5-cm dice. Peel the onions, and cut each onion lengthwise into 6 wedges.

Divide the fish and vegetables evenly between 8 presoaked wooden skewers and arrange on the broiler pan.

Mix the oregano and oil together in a small bowl. Season to taste with pepper. Lightly brush the kabobs with the oil and cook under the preheated broiler for 10–15 minutes or until evenly cooked, turning occasionally. If you cannot fit all the kabobs on the broiler pan at once, cook them in batches, keeping the cooked kabobs warm while cooking the remainder. Alternatively, these kabobs can be cooked on a barbecue.

Garnish with lime wedges and serve with salad greens.

Calories: 371   Fat: 20g   Sat Fat: 3.7g   Salt: 1.0g

Sweet & Sour Seabass

serves 2

scant ¾ cup shredded bok choy

¾ cup bean sprouts

⅔ cup sliced shiitake mushrooms

⅔ cup torn oyster mushrooms

¼ cup thinly sliced scallions

1 tsp finely grated fresh ginger

1 tbsp thinly sliced lemongrass

ready-made low-fat sweet and sour sauce

2 x 3¼-oz/2 x 90-g/ sea bass fillets, skinned

1½ tsp sesame seeds, toasted

Preheat the oven to 400°F/200°C. Cut 2 x 15-inch/38-cm squares of wax paper and 2 foil squares the same size.

Combine the bok choy, bean sprouts, both kinds of mushrooms, and the scallions in a bowl, then add the ginger and lemongrass. Toss all the ingredients together.

Put a square of wax paper on top of a square of foil and fold into a triangle. Open up and place half the vegetable mixture into the center, pour half the sweet and sour sauce over the vegetables, and place the fish fillet on top. Sprinkle with a few sesame seeds. Fold the foil to make a secure parcel. Repeat to make the second parcel.

Place the parcels on a cookie sheet and bake for 10 minutes, until the foil parcels puff with steam. To serve, place on individual plates and snip open at the table so that you can enjoy the wonderful aromas as the parcels are opened.

Calories: 150   Fat: 3g   Sat Fat: 0.5g   Salt: 0.05g

Flounder Parcels with Fresh Herbs

serves 4

vegetable oil spray

4 flounder fillets, skinned

6 tbsp chopped fresh herbs, such as dill, parsley, chives, thyme, or marjoram

finely grated rind and juice of 2 lemons

1 small onion, sliced thinly

1 tbsp capers, rinsed (optional)

salt and pepper

Preheat the oven to 375°F/190°C. Cut 4 large squares of aluminum foil, each large enough to hold a fish and form a parcel, and spray with oil.

Place each fish fillet on a foil sheet and sprinkle them with the herbs, lemon rind and juice, onion, capers, if using, salt and pepper. Fold the foil to make a secure parcel and place on a cookie sheet.

Bake the parcels in the oven for 15 minutes, or until tender. Serve the fish piping hot, in their loosely opened parcels.

Calories: 129   Fat: 2g   Sat Fat: 0.4g   Salt: 0.3g

Shrimp Risotto

serves 2

1 tsp butter

2 shallots, finely chopped

1 stick celery stalk, finely chopped

3½ oz/100 g Arborio or other risotto rice

7 fl oz/200 ml hot vegetable or fish stock

3½ fl oz/100 ml hot water

3½ fl oz/100 ml white wine

5½ oz/150 g frozen shrimp, defrosted

4 tsp chopped fresh parsley

1 tbsp low-fat crème fraîche

dash of lemon juice

pepper

1 tsp fresh Parmesan, to serve

mixed side salad with oil-free French dressing, to serve

Heat the butter in a medium nonstick skillet over a medium heat. When the butter is hot, add the shallots and celery, and cook, stirring continuously, for 3–4 minutes until softened.

Add the rice and seasoning to the frying pan and stir well to coat the rice. Mix the stock and the water. Add just enough of the stock and water mixture to cover the rice and continue to cook, stirring frequently, until it is almost completely absorbed. Continue adding the stock and water in this way until it is almost completely absorbed. Add the wine and continue cooking until that is absorbed.

Stir the shrimp and half the parsley into the risotto and heat through.

Add the crème fraîche and lemon juice, stir, and serve immediately with the cheese and the remaining parsley sprinkled over. Accompany with a large mixed side salad with an oil-free French dressing.

| Calories: 340 | Fat: 6.4g | Sat Fat: 1.9g | Salt: 1.5g |

Seafood Stir-Fry

serves 4

4 oz/115 g white fish, such as monkfish fillet

2 sprays sunflower oil

1 fresh jalapeño chile, seeded and finely chopped

1-inch/2.5-cm piece fresh ginger, peeled and grated

3 oz/85 g raw shrimp, peeled and deveined

4 oz/115 g baby corn, sliced in half lengthwise

4 oz/115 g snow peas, trimmed

6 scallions, trimmed and chopped

1 tbsp soy sauce

4 oz/115 g squid, cleaned and cut into thin slices

4 oz/115 g fresh spinach leaves

¾ cup bean sprouts

Discard any skin from the white fish, rinse lightly, and pat dry on paper towels. Cut into small pieces.

Heat a wok and when hot, add the oil and heat for 10 seconds. Add the chile and ginger and stir-fry for 1 minute then add the white fish and shrimp and stir-fry for 2 minutes.

Add the baby corn, snow peas, scallions, and soy sauce and continue to stir-fry for 2–3 minutes, or until the fish is just cooked and the shrimp have almost turned completely pink.

Add the squid, spinach, and bean sprouts and continue to stir-fry for an additional 2 minutes, or until the fish, shrimp, and squid are cooked. Serve immediately, divided equally among 4 warmed bowls.

| Calories: 172 | Fat: 2.9g | Sat Fat: 0.4g | Salt: 1.7g |

Seared Scallops

serves 4

10½ oz/300 g fresh scallops

1 tsp sunflower oil

2-inch/5-cm piece fresh ginger, peeled and grated

1 tbsp finely grated lime rind

1 orange bell pepper, seeded and sliced

1 red onion, thinly sliced

4 oz/115 g wild mushrooms, such as chanterelle, or cremini mushrooms

¼ cup lime juice

1 tsp honey (optional)

1 tbsp soy sauce

4 oz/115 g bok choy, shredded

Lightly rinse the scallops, discarding any thin black veins. Pat dry with paper towels and set aside.

Heat a wok and, when hot, add the oil. Add the grated ginger and cook, stirring for 1 minute.

Add the lime rind, bell pepper slices, and onion and stir-fry for 3–4 minutes, or until the onion has softened.

Add the scallops and mushrooms to the wok and stir-fry for 2 minutes. Make sure that the scallops are turned over after 1 minute.

Pour in the lime juice, add the honey, if using, and the soy sauce. Stir together, then add the bok choy and continue to cook for 2–3 minutes, or until the scallops are tender. Serve immediately, divided equally among 4 warmed bowls.

| Calories: 107 | Fat: 4.3g | Sat Fat: 0.6g | Salt: 1.0g |

Vegetarian Mains

Corn & Green Bean-Filled Baked Sweet Potato

serves 4

4 red-fleshed sweet potatoes, about 9 oz/250 g each

1 cup frozen fava beans

scant ¾ cup frozen corn kernels

4 oz/115 g fine long green beans

1 tbsp olive oil

1 tbsp balsamic vinegar

5 oz/140 g tomatoes

2 tbsp torn fresh basil leaves, plus extra leaves to garnish

pepper

Preheat the oven to 375°F/190°C. Scrub the sweet potatoes and pierce the skin of each potato with a sharp knife several times. Arrange on a baking sheet and bake in the preheated oven for 1–1¼ hours, or until soft and tender when pierced with the point of a sharp knife. Keep warm.

When the potatoes are cooked, bring a pan of water to a boil, add the fava beans and corn, and return to a boil. Reduce the heat, cover, and let simmer for 5 minutes. Trim the green beans, cut in half, and add to the pan. Return to a boil, then reduce the heat, cover, and let simmer for 3 minutes, or until the green beans are just tender.

Blend the oil with the vinegar in a small bowl and season to taste with pepper. Drain the corn and beans, return to the pan, add the tomatoes, and pour the dressing over. Add the torn basil leaves and mix well.

Remove the sweet potatoes from the oven, cut in half lengthwise, and open up. Divide the corn and bean filling between the potatoes and serve at once, garnished with basil leaves.

Calories: 362   Fat: 4.2g   Sat Fat: 0.1g   Salt: 0.3g

Vegetable & Filo Pie

serves 4

6 oz/175 g carrots, peeled and chopped

5 oz/140 g head of broccoli, divided into small florets

4 oz/115 g fava beans

scant ½ cup frozen or canned corn kernels

1¼ cups vegetable stock

1 tbsp cornstarch

2 tbsp water

1 tbsp chopped fresh cilantro

3 sheets filo dough

pepper

Preheat the oven to 375°F/190°C. Cook the carrots in a pan of boiling water for 6 minutes, then add the broccoli florets with the fava beans and cook for an additional 2 minutes. Stir in the corn, mix then drain thoroughly and set aside.

Heat the stock in another pan, add the vegetables, and bring to boiling point. Blend the cornstarch with the water in a bowl and stir the paste into the boiling liquid. Cook, stirring, until the sauce thickens. Stir in the chopped cilantro and add pepper to taste. Spoon the mixture into a 5-cup/1.2-liter pie dish and let cool.

Place the filo dough on the counter and brush one sheet lightly with a little water. Put a second sheet on top. Place the filo dough over the filling, pressing the edges over the filling to encase completely.

Brush the top of the pie with a little water and put the remaining sheet of dough decoratively on top. Bake for 25 minutes, or until the top is golden brown. Serve a quarter of the pie per person.

Calories: 139   Fat: 5.7g   Sat Fat: 1.8g   Salt: 0.3g

Roasted Butternut Squash

serves 4

1 butternut squash, about 1 lb/450 g

1 onion, chopped

2–3 garlic cloves, crushed

4 small tomatoes, chopped

3 oz/85 g cremini mushrooms, chopped

3 oz/85 g canned lima beans, drained, rinsed, and coarsely chopped

1 zucchini, about 4 oz/115 g, trimmed and grated

1 tbsp chopped fresh oregano, plus extra to garnish

pepper

2 tbsp tomato paste

1¼ cups water

4 scallions, trimmed and chopped

1 tbsp Worcestershire or hot pepper sauce, or to taste

Preheat the oven to 375°F/190°C. Prick the squash all over with a metal skewer then roast for 40 minutes, or until tender. Remove from the oven and leave until cool enough to handle.

Cut the squash in half, scoop out and discard the seeds then scoop out some of the flesh, making hollows in both halves. Chop the cooked flesh and put in a bowl. Place the two halves side by side in a large roasting pan.

Add the onion, garlic, chopped tomatoes, and mushrooms to the cooked squash flesh. Add the coarsely chopped lima beans, grated zucchini, chopped oregano, and pepper to taste and mix well. Spoon the filling into the 2 halves of the squash, packing it down as firmly as possible.

Mix the tomato paste with the water, scallions, and Worcestershire sauce in a small bowl and pour around the squash.

Cover loosely with a large sheet of foil and bake for 30 minutes, or until piping hot. Serve, divided equally among 4 warmed plates, garnished with extra chopped oregano.

| Calories: 62 | Fat: 0.8g | Sat Fat: 0.2g | Salt: 0.5g |

Chinese Vegetables & Bean Sprouts with Noodles

serves 4

5 cups vegetable stock

1 garlic clove, crushed

½-inch/1-cm piece fresh
ginger, finely chopped

8 oz/225 g dried medium
egg noodles

1 red bell pepper, seeded
and sliced

¾ cup frozen peas

4 oz/115 g broccoli florets

3 oz/85 g shiitake
mushrooms, sliced

2 tbsp sesame seeds

8 oz/225 g canned water
chestnuts, drained and
halved

8 oz/225 g canned bamboo
shoots, drained

10 oz/280 g Napa cabbage,
sliced

scant 1 cup bean sprouts

3 scallions, sliced

soy sauce, to taste

pepper

Bring the stock, garlic, and ginger to a boil in a large pan. Stir in the noodles, red bell pepper, peas, broccoli, and mushrooms and return to a boil. Reduce the heat, cover, and let simmer for 5–6 minutes, or until the noodles are tender.

Meanwhile, preheat the broiler to medium. Spread the sesame seeds out in a single layer on a baking sheet and toast under the preheated broiler, turning to brown evenly—watch constantly because they brown very quickly. Tip the sesame seeds into a small dish and set aside.

Once the noodles are tender, add the water chestnuts, bamboo shoots, Napa cabbage, bean sprouts, and scallions to the pan. Return the stock to a boil, stir to mix the ingredients, and let simmer for an additional 2–3 minutes to heat through thoroughly.

Carefully drain off 1¼ cups of the stock into a small heatproof pitcher and set aside. Drain and discard any remaining stock and turn the noodles and vegetables into a warmed serving dish. Quickly mix the soy sauce with the reserved stock and pour over the noodles and vegetables. Season to taste with pepper and serve at once.

| Calories: 120 | Fat: 2.8g | Sat Fat: 0.6g | Salt: 0.2g |

Vegetable Gratin

serves 1

7 oz/200 g canned chopped tomatoes

scant ¾ cup sliced button mushrooms,

⅓ cup fresh or frozen fava beans

¾ cup diced butternut squash

1 zucchini, cut into ¼-inch/ 5-mm slices

2 scallions, finely chopped

few fresh basil leaves (optional)

½ oz/15 g reduced-fat hard cheese, such as sharp cheddar, or a vegetarian Parmesan or romano

1 tbsp fresh breadcrumbs

pepper

Put the tomatoes, mushrooms, beans, and squash into a pan, bring to a simmer, cover, and simmer over low heat for 15 minutes.

Add the zucchini and scallions and cook for an additional 5–10 minutes, or until tender, adding a little water if the chopped tomatoes don't cover all the vegetables.

Meanwhile, preheat the broiler. Season to taste with pepper, stir in the basil, if using, then tip the mixture into a gratin dish, and smooth out. Combine the cheese and breadcrumbs and sprinkle them over the top. Brown under a hot broiler for 1–2 minutes, until golden. Serve immediately.

Calories: 180   Fat: 3.9g   Sat Fat: 1.6g   Salt: 0.5g

Chili Beans

serves 4–6

7 oz/200 g dried mixed beans, such as kidney, soy, pinto, cannellini, and chickpeas

1 red onion, diced

1 garlic clove, crushed

1 tbsp hot chili powder

14 oz/400 g canned chopped tomatoes in tomato juice

1 tbsp tomato paste

4 tbsp low-fat plain yogurt

soft flour tortilla wraps, to serve

Soak the beans overnight or for 8 hours in a large bowl of cold water. Drain, rinse, and put the beans into a large pan. Cover well with cold water, then bring to a boil and boil rapidly for 10 minutes. Reduce the heat, cover, and let simmer for an additional 45 minutes, or until tender. Drain.

Put the cooked beans, onion, garlic, chili powder, tomatoes, and tomato paste into a pan and bring to a boil. Reduce the heat, cover, and let simmer for 20–25 minutes, or until the onion is tender.

Ladle the chili into bowls and top with a tablespoon of yogurt. Serve immediately with soft flour tortilla wraps.

| Calories: 53 | Fat: 0.5g | Sat Fat: 0.05g | Salt: 1.3g |

Pasta with Spiced Leek, Butternut Squash & Cherry Tomatoes

serves 4

1⅓ cups sliced baby leeks

1⅓ cups diced butternut squash

1½ tbsp medium curry paste

1 tsp canola or vegetable oil

6 oz/175 g cherry tomatoes

2¼ cups dried pasta shapes

1¼ cups white sauce

2 tbsp chopped fresh cilantro leaves

Preheat the oven to 400°F/200°C. Bring a large pan of water to a boil, add the leeks, and cook for 2 minutes. Add the butternut squash and cook for 2 minutes more. Drain in a colander.

Combine the curry paste and oil in a large bowl. Add the leeks and butternut squash and toss to coat thoroughly. Transfer the leeks and butternut squash to a nonstick cookie sheet and roast for 10 minutes, until golden brown. Add the tomatoes and roast for an additional 5 minutes.

Meanwhile, cook the pasta according to the package directions, then drain. Put the white sauce into a large pan and warm over low heat. Add the leeks, butternut squash, tomatoes, and cilantro and stir in the warm pasta. Mix thoroughly and serve.

Calories: 291   Fat: 3g   Sat Fat: 0.5g   Salt: 0.25g

Penne Primavera

serves 4

1 cup baby corn

½ cup whole baby carrots

1¼ cups shelled fava beans

generous 1 cup whole green beans, cut into 1-inch/2.5-cm pieces

3 cups dried penne

1¼ cups low-fat plain yogurt

1 tbsp chopped fresh parsley

1 tbsp chopped fresh chives

salt and pepper

a few fresh chives, to garnish

Cook the corn and carrots in boiling salted water for 5 minutes, or until tender, then drain, and rinse under cold running water. Cook the fava beans and green beans in boiling salted water for 3–4 minutes, or until tender, then drain, and rinse under cold running water. If you like, slip the skins off the fava beans.

Cook the pasta in a large pan of boiling salted water for 10 minutes or as directed on the package, until tender.

Meanwhile, put the yogurt, parsley, chopped chives, salt, and pepper in a bowl and mix together.

Drain the cooked pasta and return to the pan. Add the vegetables and yogurt sauce, heat gently, and toss together, until hot.

Serve garnished with a few lengths of chives.

| Calories: 398 | Fat: 3g | Sat Fat: 1g | Salt: 1.0g |

Spring Vegetable Risotto

serves 4

3¾ cups vegetable stock

2 tsp olive oil

1 small leek, thinly sliced

1 tsp chopped garlic

1 carrot, thinly sliced

2 zucchini, thinly sliced

¾ cup snow peas

¾ cup whole green beans, cut into 1-inch/2.5-cm pieces

3 cups risotto rice

⅔ cup dry white wine

½ cup frozen baby peas, thawed

salt and pepper

Pour the stock into a pan, bring to a boil, then keep at barely simmering point.

Meanwhile, heat the oil in a large, nonstick pan, add the leek, garlic, carrot, zucchini, snow peas, and beans, and cook, stirring frequently, for 5 minutes, or until beginning to soften but not brown.

Add the rice and stir well for 2–3 minutes, or until coated in the oil. Add the wine and cook, stirring, until almost evaporated.

Add about ⅔ cup of the stock and cook gently, stirring occasionally, until absorbed. Add more stock, in ⅔-cup measures, as soon as each measure has been absorbed, stirring frequently. Continue until the rice is thick, creamy and tender.

This will take 20–25 minutes. Stir in the peas, season with salt and pepper, and serve.

Calories: 542	Fat: 7.0g	Sat Fat: 1.5g	Salt: 0.04g

Quick Mushroom Risotto

serves 1

1 tbsp dried porcini mushrooms

1 tsp olive oil

1 tsp butter

½ onion, finely chopped

1 small garlic clove, finely chopped

2¼ cups mixed fresh mushrooms (e.g. cremini, shiitake, white)

⅓ cup risotto rice

scant 1 cup vegetable stock

¼ cup dry white wine or extra stock

1 small zucchini, chopped

1 tsp chopped fresh parsley

1 tsp freshly grated vegetarian Parmesan or romano cheese

pepper

Put the dried mushrooms in a bowl, cover with water, and let soak for 30 minutes.

About 5 minutes before the soaking time is up, heat the oil and butter in a large nonstick skillet with a lid and sauté the onion and garlic over medium heat for about 5 minutes, or until softened. Add the fresh mushrooms, season with pepper, stir well, and cook for 1–2 minutes.

Add the rice and soaked mushrooms with their soaking water, stock, and wine, if using, and stir. Cover and simmer for 20 minutes, adding a little extra stock or water if it looks dry. Add the zucchini and continue to simmer for an additional 10 minutes. When the rice is tender and creamy, stir in the parsley and cheese.

Calories: 435	Fat: 11.4g	Sat Fat: 4.5g	Salt: 0.7g

Sweet Potato Curry with Lentils

serves 1

1 tsp vegetable oil

⅓ cup diced sweet potato

generous ¼ cup diced potato

1 small onion, finely chopped

1 small garlic clove, finely chopped

1 small green chile, seeded and chopped

½ tsp ground ginger

scant ¼ cup green lentils

5–7 tbsp hot vegetable stock

½ tsp garam masala

5–7 tbsp hot water (optional)

1 tbsp low-fat plain yogurt

pepper

Heat the oil in a nonstick pan with a lid and sauté the sweet potato over medium heat, turning occasionally, for 5 minutes.

Meanwhile, put the potato into a pan of water, bring to a boil, and simmer for about 6 minutes, until almost cooked. Drain and set aside. When the sweet potato cubes are sautéed, remove them with a slotted spoon. Add the onion to the pan and cook, stirring occasionally, for 5 minutes, or until translucent. Add the garlic, chile, and ginger and stir for 1 minute.

Return the sweet potato to the pan and add the boiled potato, lentils, half the stock, pepper to taste, and the garam masala. Stir well to combine, bring to a simmer, and cover.

Reduce the heat and simmer for 20 minutes, adding a little more stock if the curry looks too dry. Stir in the yogurt and serve.

Calories: 315   Fat: 4.9g   Sat Fat: 0.9g   Salt: 0.4g

Rustic Roasted Ratatouille & Potato Wedges

serves 4

10½ oz/300 g potatoes

7 oz/200 g eggplant, cut into wedges

4½ oz/125 g red onion, sliced into rings

7 oz/200 g seeded mixed bell peppers, sliced

6 oz/175 g zucchini, sliced

4½ oz/125 g cherry tomatoes

scant ½ cup low-fat cream cheese

1 tsp honey

pinch of smoked paprika

1 tsp chopped fresh flat-leaf parsley

for the marinade

1 tsp vegetable oil

1 tbsp lemon juice

4 tbsp white wine

1 tsp sugar

4 tbsp of chopped mixed

Preheat the oven to 400°F/200°C. Bake the potatoes in their skins for 30 minutes, then remove, and cut into wedges—the flesh should not be completely cooked.

To make the marinade, put all the ingredients in a bowl and blend together with a hand-held blender until smooth, or process in a food processor.

Put the potato wedges into a large bowl with the eggplant, onion, bell peppers, and zucchini, pour the marinade over the vegetables, and mix thoroughly.

Spread out the vegetables on a nonstick baking sheet and roast, turning occasionally, for 25–30 minutes, or until golden brown and tender. Add the tomatoes for the last 5 minutes of the cooking time just to split the skins and warm slightly.

Combine the cream cheese, honey, and paprika in a bowl. Serve the vegetables with a little of the cream cheese mixture, sprinkled with chopped parsley.

| Calories: 200 | Fat: 3g | Sat Fat: 1g | Salt: 0.06g |

Spinach & Butternut Squash Bake

serves 2
for the baked vegetables

scant 2 cups diced
butternut squash

2 small red onions, each
cut into 8 segments

2 tsp light vegetable or
olive oil

pepper

for the white sauce

generous 1 cup skim milk

3 tbsp cornstarch

1 tsp mustard powder

1 small onion

2 small bay leaves

4 tsp freshly grated
vegetarian Parmesan or
romano cheese

4¼ oz/120 g baby spinach
leaves

for the topping

2 tbsp whole wheat
breadcrumbs

Preheat the oven to 400°F/200°C and warm an ovenproof serving dish. Arrange the squash and onions on a nonstick baking sheet, coat with the oil and season with plenty of pepper. Bake for 20 minutes, turning once.

To make the sauce, put the milk into a small nonstick pan with the cornstarch, mustard, onion, and bay leaves. Whisk over medium heat until thick. Remove from the heat, discard the onion and bay leaves, and stir in the cheese. Set aside, stirring occasionally, to prevent a skin from forming.

When the squash is nearly cooked, put the spinach in a large pan with 1 tablespoon water and cook, stirring, for 2–3 minutes, or until just wilted.

You can continue cooking this dish in the hot oven, or preheat the broiler to medium-high. Put half the squash mixture in the warmed ovenproof dish and top with half the spinach. Repeat the layers. Pour the white sauce over the top and sprinkle with the bread crumbs. Either put under the preheated broiler until browned and bubbling, or transfer to the oven for 15–20 minutes.

Calories: 120	Fat: 3.9g	Sat Fat: 1.4g	Salt: 0.4g

Tofu Moussaka

serves 4

4 x 5 oz/150 g baking potatoes

4 tbsp lemon juice

1 tsp canola or vegetable oil

1 tsp sugar

2 tsp crushed garlic

1 tsp ground cumin

2 tbsp dried oregano

1 cup diced eggplant

3½ oz/100 g onion, sliced

¾ cup diced mixed bell peppers

7 oz/200 g canned chopped tomatoes

1¾ cups whole plain yogurt

2 tbsp cornstarch

2 tbsp mustard powder

7 oz/200 g silken tofu, sliced

3 oz/85 g beefsteak tomatoes, cut into ⅛-inch/3-mm slices

Preheat the oven to 375°F/190°C. Bake the potatoes in their skins for 45 minutes, then remove, and cut into ⅛-inch/3-mm slices.

Combine the lemon juice, oil, sugar, garlic, cumin, and oregano in a small bowl, then lightly brush the mixture over the diced eggplant, reserving the remaining mixture. Spread out the eggplant on a nonstick baking sheet and bake for 15 minutes.

Heat the reserved lemon juice mixture in a small pan over high heat, add the onion and bell peppers, and cook, stirring occasionally, until lightly browned. Add the canned tomatoes, reduce the heat, and simmer for 4 minutes.

Whisk the yogurt and cornstarch together in another pan, then bring to the boil, whisking constantly until the yogurt boils and thickens (you must whisk constantly or the yogurt will separate before thickening). When the yogurt has thickened, remove from the heat and whisk in the mustard powder.

Make as many separate layers of the ingredients as you can in an ovenproof dish, alternating with the sauce: tofu, sauce, onion and bell peppers, sauce, eggplant, sauce, potato, sauce, and tofu, then finish with a layer of beefsteak tomato topped with sauce. Bake for 20–25 minutes, or until golden brown on top.

| Calories: 255 | Fat: 5.5g | Sat Fat: 1g | Salt: 0.3g |

Mushroom Stroganoff

serves 4

1 lb 4 oz/550 g mixed fresh mushrooms, such as cremini, chanterelles, porcini, and oyster

1 red onion, diced

2 garlic cloves, crushed

scant 2 cups vegetable stock

1 tbsp tomato paste

2 tbsp lemon juice

scant 1 tbsp cornstarch

2 tbsp cold water

½ cup low-fat plain yogurt

3 tbsp chopped fresh flat-leaf parsley

freshly ground black pepper

boiled brown or white rice and crisp green salad, to serve

Put the mushrooms, onion, garlic, stock, tomato paste, and lemon juice into a pan and bring to a boil. Reduce the heat, cover, and let simmer for 15 minutes, or until the onion is tender.

Blend the cornstarch with the water in a small bowl and stir into the mushroom mixture. Return to a boil, stirring constantly, and cook until the sauce thickens. Reduce the heat and let simmer for an additional 2–3 minutes, stirring occasionally.

Just before serving, remove the pan from the heat, and stir in the yogurt, making sure that the stroganoff is not boiling or it may separate and curdle. Stir in 2 tablespoons of the parsley and season to taste with pepper. Transfer the stroganoff to a warmed serving dish, sprinkle over the remaining parsley, and serve at once with boiled brown or white rice and a crisp green salad.

| Calories: 87 | Fat: 1.2g | Sat Fat: 0.5g | Salt: 0.1g |

Vegetable & Tofu Stir-Fry

serves 4

8 oz/225 g firm tofu (drained weight), cut into bite-size pieces

1 tbsp peanut or corn oil

2 scallions, chopped

1 garlic clove, finely chopped

4 oz/115 g baby corn, halved

1 cup snow peas

4 oz/115 g shiitake mushrooms, thinly sliced

2 tbsp finely chopped fresh cilantro leaves

for the marinade

2 tbsp dark soy sauce

1 tbsp Chinese rice wine

2 tsp brown sugar

½ tsp Chinese five-spice powder

1 fresh red chile, seeded and finely chopped

2 scallions, finely chopped

1 tbsp grated fresh ginger

Place all the marinade ingredients in a large, shallow, nonmetallic dish and stir to mix. Add the bite-size chunks of tofu and turn them over carefully to coat thoroughly in the marinade. Cover the dish with plastic wrap and leave the tofu in the refrigerator to marinate for 2 hours, turning the chunks over once or twice.

Drain the tofu and set aside the marinade. Heat the peanut oil in a preheated wok or large skillet. Add the tofu and stir-fry over medium-high heat for 2–3 minutes, or until golden. Using a slotted spoon, remove the tofu from the wok and set aside. Add the scallions and garlic and stir-fry for 2 minutes, then add the corn cobs and stir-fry for 1 minute. Add the snow peas and mushrooms and stir-fry for an additional 2 minutes.

Return the tofu to the wok and add the marinade. Cook gently for 1–2 minutes, or until heated through. Sprinkle with the chopped fresh cilantro and serve immediately.

Calories: 135   Fat: 7g   Sat Fat: 3g   Salt: 0.7g

Moroccan Vegetable Stew

serves 4

15 oz/425 g canned chickpeas

4 tomatoes, peeled and seeded

3 cups vegetable stock

1 onion, peeled and sliced

2 carrots, peeled and sliced diagonally

1 tbsp chopped fresh cilantro

salt

6 oz/175 g zucchini, sliced

1 small turnip, peeled and cubed

½ tsp ground turmeric

¼ tsp ground ginger

¼ tsp ground cinnamon

1½ cups couscous

fresh cilantro sprigs, to garnish

Drain the chickpeas, rinse under cold running water and set aside. Coarsely chop the tomatoes and set aside half. Place the remainder in a blender or food processor and process until a smooth purée forms. Transfer to a large pan and add 1¾ cups of the vegetable stock. Bring to a boil, then reduce the heat, and add the onion, carrots, chopped fresh cilantro, and salt to taste. Let simmer, stirring occasionally, for 10 minutes.

Stir in the zucchini, turnip, turmeric, ginger, and cinnamon. Partially cover and simmer for an additional 30 minutes. Stir in the reserved chickpeas and let simmer for a few more minutes.

Meanwhile, bring the remaining vegetable stock to the boil in a heavy-bottom pan. Add a pinch of salt, then sprinkle in the couscous, stirring constantly. Remove the pan from the heat, cover with a tight-fitting lid and let stand for 5 minutes. Fluff up the couscous with a fork and transfer to 4 large serving plates.

Top with the vegetables and their stock, garnish with a few sprigs of fresh cilantro, and serve immediately.

Calories: 299   Fat: 4g   Sat Fat: 0.8g   Salt: 0.7g

Glazed Vegetable Kabobs

serves 4

⅔ cup low-fat plain yogurt

4 tbsp mango chutney

1 tsp chopped garlic

1 tbsp lemon juice

8 baby onions, peeled

16 baby corn, halved

2 zucchini, cut into 1-inch/ 2.5-cm pieces

16 white mushrooms

16 cherry tomatoes

salt and pepper

salad greens, to garnish

If using wooden skewers, pre-soak them for 30 minutes to prevent burning under the broiler. Put the yogurt, chutney, garlic, lemon juice, salt, and pepper in a bowl and stir together.

Put the onions in a pan of boiling water. Return to a boil, then drain well.

Thread the onions, corn, zucchini, mushrooms, and tomatoes alternately onto 8 metal or wooden skewers.

Arrange the kabobs on a broiler pan and brush with the yogurt glaze. Cook under a preheated broiler for 10 minutes, turning and brushing frequently, until golden and tender.

Serve with a garnish of mixed salad greens.

| Calories: 144 | Fat: 1g | Sat Fat: 0.4g | Salt: 2.5g |

Desserts

Pear & Chocolate Cream

serves 1

2¾ oz/75 g drained canned pears in juice

⅓ cup low-fat cream cheese

few drops of vanilla extract

1 tbsp grated milk chocolate

Process the pears to a purée in a blender or mash thoroughly with a fork.

Combine the pears, cream cheese, and vanilla extract in a bowl, then lightly stir in two thirds of the chocolate. Spoon into a single-serving dessert glass or dish and top with the remaining chocolate. Chill before serving.

| Calories: 150 | Fat: 4.7g | Sat Fat: 2.7g | Salt: 0.1g |

Strawberry & Orange Dessert

serves 2

1¾ cups orange juice

1 tbsp powdered gelatin or vegetarian equivalent

⅔ cup sliced small strawberries

Pour scant ½ cup of the juice in a small heatproof bowl, sprinkle the gelatin over the surface, and let stand for 5 minutes. Set the bowl over a pan of simmering water and stir until the gelatin melts and the liquid becomes clear, then stir in the remaining juice.

Divide the strawberries between 2 large wine glasses. Pour in enough juice to just cover the strawberries and transfer to the refrigerator for 30 minutes, or until set. Keep the remaining juice warm, making sure that the gelatin does not set. Pour in the remaining juice and return to the refrigerator until set.

Calories: 130   Fat: 0.2g   Sat Fat: 0.0g   Salt: 0.2g

Blueberry Fools

serves 4

1 heaping tbsp custard powder

1¼ cups low-fat milk

2 tbsp superfine sugar

scant ¾ cup fresh or frozen blueberries, thawed if frozen

⅞ cup low-fat mascarpone cheese

Blend the custard powder with ¼ cup of the milk in a heatproof bowl. Bring the remaining milk to a boil in a small pan and pour over the custard mixture, mixing well. Return the custard to the pan and return to a boil over medium-low heat, stirring constantly, until thickened. Pour the custard into the bowl and sprinkle the sugar over the top of the custard to prevent a skin forming. Cover and let cool completely.

Set aside 12 blueberries for decoration. Put the remaining blueberries and cold custard into a blender and process until smooth.

Spoon the mascarpone cheese and the blueberry mixture in alternate layers into 4 tall glasses. Decorate with the reserved blueberries and serve at once.

Calories: 133   Fat: 2.8g   Sat Fat: 1.5g   Salt: 0.2g

Baked Banana with Sin-Free Chocolate Sauce

serves 1

1 small banana

2 tsp light corn syrup

3 tsp unsweetened cocoa powder

Preheat the oven to 350°F/180C°. Bake the banana in its skin for 10 minutes, or until the skin is black.

Meanwhile, warm the syrup in a small pan over medium heat for 2–3 minutes, or in a medium-low microwave for 1 minute, until very runny. Stir in the unsweetened cocoa powder until smooth and chocolate-like. Keep warm.

When the banana is cooked, discard the skin, put the flesh on a plate, pour the chocolate sauce over it, and serve.

| Calories: 140 | Fat: 2.6g | Sat Fat: 0.6g | Salt: 0.2g |

Fruity Stuffed Nectarines

serves 4

4 ripe but firm nectarines or peaches

5 oz/140 g blueberries

4 oz/115 g fresh raspberries

⅔ cup freshly squeezed orange juice

1–2 tsp honey, or to taste

1 tbsp brandy (optional)

scant 1 cup low-fat strained plain yogurt

1 tbsp finely grated orange rind

Preheat the oven to 350°F/180°C. Cut the nectarines in half and remove the pits then place in a shallow ovenproof dish.

Mix the blueberries and raspberries together in a bowl and use to fill the hollows left by the removal of the nectarine pits. Spoon any extra berries around the edge of the nectarines.

Mix together the orange juice, honey, and brandy, if using, in a small bowl and pour over the fruit. Blend the yogurt with the grated orange rind in another bowl and let chill in the refrigerator until required.

Bake the berry-filled nectarines for 10 minutes, or until the fruit is hot. Serve with the orange-flavored yogurt.

| Calories: 115 | Fat: 1.5g | Sat Fat: 0.8g | Salt: 0.1g |

Fruity Yogurt Cups

serves 4

2 cups low-fat plain yogurt

1½ tbsp finely grated orange rind

8 oz/225 g mixed berries, such as blueberries, raspberries, and strawberries, plus extra to decorate

fresh mint sprigs, to decorate (optional)

Set the freezer to rapid freeze at least 2 hours before freezing this dish. Line a 12-hole muffin pan with 12 paper cake cases, or use small ramekin dishes placed on a baking sheet.

Mix the yogurt and orange rind together in a large bowl. Cut any large strawberries into pieces so that they are the same size as the blueberries and raspberries.

Add the fruit to the yogurt then spoon into the paper cases or ramekins. Freeze for 2 hours, or until just frozen. Decorate with extra fruit and mint sprigs, if using, and serve. Remember to return the freezer to its original setting afterward.

Calories: 78   Fat: 1.2g   Sat Fat: 0.7g   Salt: 0.2g

Ruby Fruits with Baby Meringues

serves 4

for the meringues

1 egg white

scant ¼ cup superfine sugar

for the fruit

8 oz/225 g fresh or frozen raspberries

2 tsp honey

scant 1 cup water

12 oz/350 g mixed fresh fruits, such as raspberries, strawberries, and pitted cherries

few fresh mint sprigs, to decorate

Preheat the oven to 250°F/120°C and line a baking sheet with parchment paper.

Whisk the egg white in a grease-free bowl until stiff then gradually add the sugar a spoonful at a time, whisking well after each addition. When all the sugar has been added and the mixture is stiff, spoon into a pastry bag fitted with a large star tip and pipe small whirls onto the lined baking sheet. Alternatively, shape into mounds with 2 teaspoons.

Bake in the oven for 1 hour, or until crisp. Let cool before removing from the baking sheet. Store in an airtight container.

Place the raspberries in a pan with the honey and water. Bring to a boil then reduce the heat to a simmer and cook for 5–8 minutes, or until the raspberries have collapsed. Let cool for 5 minutes. Transfer to a food processor and process to form a purée.

Press the purée through a strainer, adding a little extra water if the purée is too thick.

Prepare the fresh fruits and stir into the purée. Stir until coated and serve with the baby meringues, decorated with mint sprigs.

Calories: 111	Fat: 0.3g	Sat Fat: 0.1g	Salt: 0.1g

Orange Cups

serves 4

4 large oranges

1 cup buttermilk or low-fat plain yogurt

1 tsp honey

1 tsp chocolate shavings (optional)

Set the freezer to rapid freeze at least 2 hours before freezing. To ensure that the oranges stand upright, cut a thin slice from the base of each. Cut a lid from each orange at the other end and set aside. Carefully cut down the inside of each orange and remove the pith and flesh from each. Do this over a bowl to catch all the juice.

Discard the pith from the scooped out flesh, then chop the flesh to make a chunky purée. Place in a bowl with the juice. Stir in the buttermilk and the honey, and pour into a freezerproof container. Freeze for 1 hour. Place the empty orange shells upside down on paper towels and let drain.

Remove the orange mixture from the freezer and stir well, breaking up any ice crystals. Return to the freezer for an additional 30 minutes, or until semi-frozen.

Stir again and use to fill the orange shells. Stand the filled oranges upright in a container. Freeze for an additional hour, or until frozen.

Before serving, transfer to the refrigerator for 30 minutes to soften slightly. Serve decorated with chocolate shavings, if using. Remember to return the freezer to its original setting afterward.

Calories: 83   Fat: 1.0g   Sat Fat 0.6g   Salt: 0.1g

Exotic Fruit Cocktail

serves 4

2 oranges

2 large passion fruit

1 pineapple

1 pomegranate

1 banana

Cut 1 orange in half and squeeze the juice into a bowl, discarding any pips. Using a sharp knife, cut away all the peel and pith from the second orange. Working over the bowl to catch the juice, carefully cut the orange segments between the membranes to obtain skinless segments of fruit. Discard any pips.

Cut the passion fruit in half, scoop the flesh into a nylon strainer and, using a spoon, push the pulp and juice into the bowl of orange segments. Discard the pips.

Using a sharp knife, cut away all the skin from the pineapple and cut the flesh lengthwise into quarters. Cut away the central hard core. Cut the flesh into chunks and add to the orange and passion fruit mixture. Cover and let chill the fruit at this stage if you are not serving at once.

Cut the pomegranate into quarters and, using your fingers or a teaspoon, remove the red seeds from the membrane. Cover and let chill until ready to serve—do not add too early to the fruit cocktail because the seeds discolor the other fruit.

Just before serving, peel and slice the banana, add to the fruit cocktail with the pomegranate seeds, and mix thoroughly. Serve at once.

Calories: 152   Fat: 0.9g   Sat Fat: 0.1g   Salt: 0.01g

Berry Yogurt Ice

serves 4

generous 1 cup raspberries

generous 1 cup blackberries

generous 1 cup strawberries

1 large egg

¾ cup strained plain yogurt

½ cup red wine

2¼ tsp powdered gelatin

fresh berries, to decorate

Put the raspberries, blackberries, and strawberries in a blender or food processor and process until a smooth purée forms. Press the purée through a strainer into a bowl to remove the seeds.

Break the egg and separate the yolk and white into separate bowls. Stir the egg yolk and yogurt into the berry purée and set the egg white aside.

Pour the wine into a heatproof bowl and sprinkle the gelatin on the surface. Let stand for 5 minutes to soften, then set the bowl over a pan of simmering water until the gelatin has dissolved. Pour the mixture into the berry purée in a steady stream, whisking constantly. Transfer the mixture to a freezerproof container and freeze for 2 hours, or until slushy.

Whisk the egg white in a spotlessly clean, grease-free bowl until very stiff. Remove the berry mixture from the freezer and fold in the egg white. Return to the freezer and freeze for 2 hours, or until firm. To serve, scoop the berry yogurt ice into glass dishes and decorate with fresh berries of your choice.

Calories: 118   Fat: 6g   Sat Fat: 3g   Salt: 0.1g

Coffee Ice Cream

serves 6

¾ cup strong black coffee,
cooled and chilled

1 square semi-sweet
chocolate

1 cup ricotta cheese

5 tbsp low-fat plain yogurt

⅜ cup superfine sugar

½ tsp ground cinnamon

dash of vanilla extract

generous 2 tbsp chocolate
flakes, plus extra to
decorate

Make the coffee in advance and leave in the refrigerator to chill. Grate the chocolate and set aside. Put the ricotta cheese, yogurt, and sugar in a blender or food processor and process until a smooth purée forms. Transfer to a large bowl and beat in the coffee, cinnamon, vanilla extract, and grated chocolate.

Spoon the mixture into a freezerproof container and freeze for 1½ hours, or until slushy. Remove from the freezer, turn into a bowl, and beat. Return to the container and freeze for 1½ hours.

Repeat this beating and freezing process twice more before serving in scoops, decorated with chocolate flakes. Alternatively, leave in the freezer until 15 minutes before serving, then transfer to the refrigerator to soften slightly before scooping.

Calories: 150   Fat: 6g   Sat Fat: 4g   Salt: 0.4g

Summer Pavlova

serves 6

for the meringues

2 egg whites

scant ¼ cup superfine sugar

1 tsp cornstarch

1 tsp vanilla extract

1 tsp vinegar

for the filling

1⅓ cups low-fat cream cheese

⅔ cup low-fat plain yogurt

½–1 tsp vanilla extract, or to taste

10½ oz/300 g mixed berries

Preheat the oven to 250°F/120°C and line a baking sheet with nonstick parchment paper. Whisk the egg whites in a grease-free bowl until stiff then gradually add the sugar a spoonful at a time, whisking well after each addition. Stir in the cornstarch, vanilla extract, and the vinegar.

When all the sugar has been added and the mixture is stiff, spoon onto the lined baking sheet and form into a 6-inch/15-cm circle, hollowing out the center to form a case.

Bake in the oven for 1½–2 hours, or until crisp. Switch the oven off and let cool in the oven. Remove from the oven and leave until cold before removing from the baking sheet. Store in an airtight container until required.

Beat the cream cheese and yogurt together in a bowl until well blended, then stir in the vanilla extract. Clean the fruits if necessary, cutting any large fruits into bite-size pieces. When ready to serve, pile the cheese filling in the center of the pavlova case, top with the fruits, and serve cut into 6 slices.

| Calories: 167 | Fat: 10g | Sat Fat: 7g | Salt: 0.4g |

Chocolate Swiss Roll

serves 12

3 eggs

heaping ⅓ cup superfine sugar, plus extra for sprinkling

1 tbsp unsweetened cocoa

scant 1 cup self-rising flour

1 tbsp boiled water, cooled

for the filling

1 cup cottage cheese or low-fat cream cheese

1 tbsp finely grated orange rind

2 tsp honey

Preheat the oven to 425°F/220°C. Line a 12 x 9-inch/ 30 x 23-cm jelly roll pan with nonstick parchment paper. Cut 2 more sheets of the same size and reserve.

Break the eggs into a heatproof bowl and add the sugar. Place the bowl over a pan of simmering water and whisk until the whisk leaves a trail when dragged across the surface. Remove from the heat and whisk until cool.

Sift the cocoa and flour together in a separate bowl, then stir lightly into the egg mixture. Add the cooled boiled water, stir, then pour into the prepared pan. Tap the pan lightly on the counter to remove any air bubbles.

Bake for 8–10 minutes, or until the top springs back lightly when touched. Remove from the oven. Invert the cake onto one of the reserved sheets of parchment paper, sprinkled with superfine sugar. Remove the pan and carefully strip off the parchment paper. Place the other reserved sheet of paper on top then carefully roll up and leave until cold.

To make the filling, beat the cheese, orange rind, and honey together in a bowl. When the jelly roll is cold unroll and spread with the cottage cheese mixture, then carefully roll up. Trim the edges and serve cut into thin slices.

Calories: 102   Fat: 2.6g   Sat Fat: 1.0g   Salt: 0.3g

Mango Cheesecakes

serves 4

corn oil, for oiling

2 tbsp polyunsaturated spread

½ tsp ground ginger

⅝ cup rolled oats

1 large ripe mango, about 1 lb 5 oz/600 g

1⅛ cups virtually fat-free Quark soft cheese

scant ½ cup medium-fat soft cheese

12 raspberries, to decorate (optional)

Line the bottom and sides of 4 x ⅔-cup ramekins with wax paper and very lightly oil.

Melt the spread in a small pan over low heat, remove from the heat, and stir in the ginger and oats. Mix thoroughly and let cool.

Using a sharp knife, cut the mango lengthwise down either side of the thin central seed. Peel the skin. Cut away any flesh from around the seed. Cut the flesh into chunks and set aside 4 oz/115 g. Put the remaining mango flesh into a food processor or blender and process until smooth. Transfer to a small bowl.

Drain away any excess fluid from the cheeses and, using a fork or tablespoon, blend together in a bowl. Finely chop the reserved mango flesh and stir into the cheese mixture along with 1 tablespoon of the mango purée. Divide the cheesecake filling evenly between the ramekins and level with the back of a spoon. Cover each cheesecake evenly with the cooled oat mixture and let chill in the refrigerator for at least 3 hours for the filling to firm. Cover and let chill with the mango purée.

To serve, carefully trim the lining paper level with the oat mixture. Since the oat base is crumbly, place an individual serving plate on top of a ramekin when turning out the cheesecakes. Holding both ramekin and plate firmly, turn over to invert. Carefully remove the ramekin and peel away the lining paper. Repeat for the remaining cheesecakes. Spoon the mango purée around each cheesecake and decorate the top of each with 3 raspberries, if using. Serve at once.

| Calories: 259 | Fat: 12g | Sat Fat: 3.8g | Salt: 0.4g |

Apricot Oatbars

makes 10

corn oil, for oiling

6 oz/175 g polyunsaturated spread

scant ½ cup raw brown sugar

⅛ cup honey

scant 1 cup dried apricots, chopped

2 tsp sesame seeds

2½ cups rolled oats

Preheat the oven to 350°F/180°C. Very lightly oil a 10½ x 6½-inch/26 x 17-cm shallow baking pan.

Put the spread, sugar, and honey into a small pan over low heat and heat until the ingredients have melted together—do not boil. When the ingredients are warm and well combined, stir in the apricots, sesame seeds, and oats.

Spoon the mixture into the prepared pan and lightly level with the back of a spoon. Cook in the preheated oven for 20–25 minutes, or until golden brown. Remove from the oven, cut into 10 bars, and let cool completely before removing from the baking pan. Store the oatbars in an airtight container and consume within 2–3 days.

| Calories: 293 | Fat: 16.5g | Sat Fat: 2.9g | Salt: 0.4g |

Peach & Apple Crumble

serves 4–5

1 cooking apple

2 eating apples

½ cup cold water

14 oz/400 g canned peach slices in fruit juice, drained

for the crumble

scant ⅝ cup all-purpose flour

⅝ cup rolled oats

generous ¼ cup firmly packed raw brown sugar

2 oz/55 g polyunsaturated spread

custard made with low-fat milk, low-fat plain mascarpone cheese, or yogurt, to serve

Preheat the oven to 375°F/190°C. Peel, core, and slice the apples and put into a small pan with the water. Bring to a boil, then cover and let simmer, stirring occasionally, for 4–5 minutes, or until just tender. Remove from the heat and drain away any excess liquid. Stir the drained peach slices into the apple and transfer the fruit to an ovenproof dish.

Meanwhile, combine the flour, oats, and sugar in a mixing bowl. Rub in the spread with your fingertips until the mixture resembles fine breadcrumbs.

Sprinkle the crumble topping evenly over the fruit and bake in the preheated oven for 20 minutes, or until golden brown. Serve warm with custard made with low-fat milk, or low-fat plain mascarpone cheese, or yogurt. This dessert is best eaten on the day it is made—any leftover crumble should be stored in the refrigerator and consumed within 24 hours.

Calories: 315   Fat: 9.9g   Sat Fat: 1.8g   Salt: 0.3g

Golden Raisin Tealoaf

*Makes one 1 lb/
450 g loaf – 10–12 slices*

corn oil, for oiling

scant ½ cup bran flakes

⅔ cup golden raisins

scant ½ cup firmly packed
raw brown sugar

1¼ cups low-fat milk

scant 1½ cups self-rising
flour

tea or freshly squeezed
fruit juice, to serve

Very lightly oil a 1-lb/450-g loaf pan and line the bottom with waxed paper.

Put the bran flakes, golden raisins, sugar, and milk into a mixing bowl, cover, and let soak for at least 1 hour in the refrigerator, or until the bran flakes have softened and the fruit has plumped up after absorbing some of the milk—the mixture can be left overnight in the refrigerator.

Preheat the oven to 375°F/190°C. Stir the flour into the soaked ingredients, mix well, and spoon into the loaf pan. Bake in the preheated oven for 40–45 minutes, or until the point of a sharp knife inserted into the center of the loaf comes out clean. Let cool in the pan on a wire rack.

When cold, turn the loaf out, and discard the lining paper. Serve in slices with cups of tea or glasses of freshly squeezed fruit juice. Store any leftover loaf in an airtight container and consume within 2–3 days.

| Calories: 156 | Fat: 1.3g | Sat Fat: 0.5g | Salt: 0.3g |

Virtually Fat-Free Marble Cake

serves 8

corn oil, for brushing

generous ¾ cup all-purpose flour, sifted, plus extra for dusting

3 tbsp unsweetened cocoa

generous 1 cup superfine sugar

pinch of salt

10 egg whites

1 tsp cream of tartar

½ tsp almond extract

½ tsp vanilla extract

confectioners' sugar, for dusting

Preheat the oven to 350°F/180°C. Oil and dust an 8-inch/20-cm deep cake pan. Sift ⅓ cup of the flour with the unsweetened cocoa and 2 tablespoons of the sugar into a bowl 4 times. Sift the remaining flour with 2 tablespoons of the sugar and the salt into a separate bowl 4 times.

Beat the egg whites in a spotlessly clean, grease-free bowl until soft peaks form. Add the cream of tartar and beat in the remaining superfine sugar.

Adding 1 tablespoonful at a time, beat until the egg whites form stiff peaks. Whisk in the almond and vanilla extracts. Divide the mixture in half. Fold the cocoa and flour mixture into one half and the unflavored flour into the other half. Spoon the cocoa flavored mixture into the pan and top with the unflavored mixture. Run a round-bladed knife through both mixtures to create a marbled effect.

Bake in the preheated oven for 45 minutes, or until the tip of a knife inserted into the center of the cake comes out clean. Invert onto a wire rack to cool and dust with confectioners' sugar before serving.

Calories: 186   Fat: 1g   Sat Fat: 1g   Salt: 0.2g